Reveries at Stillmeadow

A Woman's Precious Moments From The Stillmeadow Books of
Gladys Taber

Selected by Peter Seymour
Illustrated by Stewart Sherwood

HALLMARK EDITIONS

This edition published by special arrangement
with J. B. Lippincott Company, Philadelphia
and New York. Printed in the United
States of America. Library of Congress Catalog
Card Number: 75-109001. Standard Book
Number: 87529-056-6.

Country Living

STILLMEADOW

'A house is not a home,' the saying goes, but Gladys Taber does have a house, a 1690 farmhouse named Stillmeadow that is a true home, 'steadfast and secure':

There is something about the task of preparing vegetables that gives a woman a reflective mood. I wondered how many tons of potatoes I had pared since we put our roots down here in these forty acres of stony Connecticut soil. The woods and fields, old orchards and brooks seem to have always been the homeplace, the cliffs and swamps and sweet hay meadows have a sense of timelessness about them.

And so does the little white farmhouse, as steadfast and secure as it was when it was built in 1690.

I went back in my memory to the early days, and decided we had more courage than sense when we bought the farm. We had faith, though. Now and then someone I meet will say, "How did you two ever decide to move to the country?"

We had, I say, a simple reason. We wanted a weekend place for our children. There were two families: [my friend] Jill and her doctor husband and their son Don and daughter Dorothy who lived in a big drafty city apartment around the corner from the tiny dark four-room sixth-floor apartment my husband and I had. With our daughter, Connie, and a cocker spaniel, our place was pretty crowded.

We all worked as hard as beavers, or harder. Jill was a top psychiatric social worker for the city, her husband never took an hour off from his practice, which was heavy, my husband taught and I was working at Columbia hoping to get the Ph.D. degree as soon as possible.

The city schools then were not as crowded as they are now, but they were not exactly spacious. After school, the children could stand around on the sidewalk or wheel their doll carriages around the block. Or we could go to the zoo and look at the other caged animals.

All three of the children were thin and pale, no matter how we stuffed them with vitamins. Also, it didn't seem to me we had much fun.

We began to dream of a weekend place where we could have outdoor living in peace and comfort where vacations and holidays could be, we felt, very economical.

And so, fortified with nothing but determination and a down payment, we turned ourselves over to Stillmeadow.

I reflected in this thinking-back hour how fortunate we were. As the children grew up and went away to their various schools and colleges, they had a home to come back to, instead of a series of transient city apartments.

And when we lost our husbands, the farm was a refuge and a haven, something to hold fast to. And something we had to work for, which was a blessing.

I often think of all the people who lived and loved, were happy or sad, those who were born in and those who died in this house. For there is a continuity of living if your house has sheltered its own down the long sweep of years.

In our turn, we have cherished it, warmed it, and it has offered us days rich with contentment. It has given us backbreaking hours of work and the satisfaction of tangible results from that work. It has given us fire on the hearth on long evenings, spring sunlight through the windows, cool moonlight on the doorsills in autumn.

This is a small house, but wide enough for fifteen cockers, two cats, an Irish setter, children growing up, friends who drop in overnight and stay three weeks.

The story of our life is written in white tulips set in the Quiet Garden, in tomatoes ripening on the vine, in puppies bouncing through the great snowdrifts. It is inscribed with the scent of dark purple lilacs, the satiny touch of eggplant, the swift falling of golden leaves.

As the seasons come to our gentle valley, Stillmeadow is always our personal adventure in happiness.

'AN OLD ORCHARD'

Baked apples, pies, sweet cider and many glorious things come from an old orchard, but the best among them is the feel of the past and the memories it evokes:

I remember the autumn day when we took a picnic lunch up the hill to the old orchard. There is an outcropping ledge there, and we spread our sandwiches and eggs on it. There is something peaceful about an old orchard. You can feel the past. The ancient apple trees were planted by some early owner of Stillmeadow; probably a father and his sons went up to clear the slope, dig the holes, set the saplings straight. The trees grew and bore russets, greenings and snow apples. From the orchard came many pies, jellies, and apples to bake, to roast over the coals, and to turn

into flaky dumplings. Sweet cider was made, too, and apple vinegar. Small boys carried apples in their pockets as they hung around the iron kettle bubbling with apple butter, dark and spicy.

Apples were sliced and strung on cords to dry in the sun. The orchard was vastly important to family living. Now the old trees still bear some fruit, and we fill the picnic basket with it. The windfalls feed the little people of the woods, squirrels like the seeds and pheasants peck happily at them. Occasionally a deer comes along. And after the autumn storms, we have applewood for burning, a final gift of beauty. I thank the man who planted our orchard.

'THE RICHES WE ACQUIRED'

Country living is indefinable in terms of estimated value. There are no price tags for secret places, ice-smooth ponds, and lanterns lit for winter outings:

The rewards of country living are measured in intangibles chiefly. Who could estimate the value of the secret places the children had in the upper woods, just when they needed secret places? Under a giant oak that has stood for a generation, a small cave is set in the cliff, and there they could set out their acorn cups for tea, leave mysterious messages for one another and generally reign in a world uncluttered by adults. Every child needs a secret place, and how few there are for city children!

The picnics we have had would stretch from here to the moon, I daresay. Spread out on sun-warmed flat gray boulders or eaten by some rush-fringed stream or cooked on the grill down by the pond, they add up to a rich store of memory.

The hot burning days when we have gone down to the pond and spent an hour swimming, the icy winter days when the children skated on clear black ice half the day, the crisp autumn days when we all went up the hill to gather butternuts and black walnuts, the spring evenings we drove around looking at the country.

No, I could never add up the riches we acquired by striking our roots firmly down into the kind earth in our little valley. Even the hard times are rewarding to a country dweller.

There is a fine sense of pride in managing when the great storms take out the "electric" and you shovel snow, lug wood for the fireplaces, light a lantern for the chores, simmer the soup in the big kettle over the embers, and have once more conquered.

And often, just as we raised our heads above

the surface of our financial problems, the roof would begin to leak, or the barn start to collapse. But after we managed each crisis, we felt more faith in being able to meet the next one.

Once, in a time of great stress, I asked Jill a question I had not dared to ask before.

"Do you ever regret moving to the country?" I asked.

She gave me a look of utter surprise.

"Every day," she said, "I thank God."

Which, after all, pretty well summed it up.

'ESPECIALLY DOGS...AND SOMETIMES CATS'

Here Miss Taber illustrates the endless lessons to be learned from the animals at Stillmeadow—lessons in laughter, responsiveness, and companionship:

One reason I love dogs is that they are without pretense. When guests come that they do not take to, they all turn cool eyes on them and retire. They do not care for people who gush or jingle keys at them or coo. They know instantly who loves them and speaks their language, and who is just pretending to make us satisfied. When Admiral Klakring and Lois came for lunch, the whole bevy mobbed them. People might be impressed by the Admiral's war record as commander of the submarine fleet in the Pacific, his fame, his citations. The dogs didn't give a fig for this. They said, in unison, these are wonderful friends!

Among the many gifts our dogs have given us, I might rate laughter as one of the best. They just naturally do funny things, from jumping in the air after wasps or grasshoppers to tunneling under the border after moles. The cockers never realize when they are funny, but the Irish has a gleam in her dark eyes as she knocks out a screen and leaps in. Didn't think I could do it, eh? she says.

Dog language is something there has been controversy about, but not by people who live with it. Holly has a wide vocabulary—for instance, mail and town. If I say, "I am going for the mail," she resigns herself with a huge sigh. This means a brief trip to the box up the hill, not worth putting on her leash, getting her into the car, getting back in the yard. But if I say, "I am going to town," she nearly knocks the door down, flies to the gate and puts her paws on the latch ready to go.

As for her own speech, I know which bark means I must stop everything and give her something to eat. The go-out bark is entirely different. Then there is the "There comes that nice boy down the road." And the earsplitting shriek, "A horse! A horse!"

I never understand why some people do not appreciate cats, but I've come to believe it is partly that they want cats to behave in a human pattern. Dogs, by and large, will do anything, no matter how silly, if their humans so desire. If you want a dog to wear rubbers when it rains, he will wear them. If you want to half-starve him and beat him, he will accept that. He will carry your slippers, fetch part of the mail from the gate, and so on.

But cats have a strong feeling for their own individuality and seldom will demean themselves. I think I should not like to see a cat not being a cat. A regimented cat would be a sorry thing.

It is not true that cats select people who hate cats and torture them by sitting on their laps. No respectable cat would care who liked him or not. It does not fit with their attitude to life in any way.

The reason they seek out the non-cat lovers is simple. Such people ignore them, do not make

cooing noises, or kitty-kitty calls, or snap fingers to get their attention. Such people, in my long observation, are almost always quiet-voiced and do not make sudden gestures. And the fact that they do not try to gather a cat up and make a fuss means the cat can make the advances.

But dogs have a sure knowledge of whether you like them or not. Cats, perhaps, assume they have to be welcomed by anybody because they are royalty. I never knew a cat that did not feel a slight condescension in making advances. The day we moved to the country was discouraging. It is not easy to have a car full of people plus a carton of puppies, three full-grown cockers, and one Siamese cat in a carrying case screaming her head off. Few cats I have known really enjoy riding in a car, especially in a carrying case. All along the road men were leaning out of cars and staring, suspecting we were murdering some innocent. One state trooper drew up alongside and looked with disbelief at the contents of the car and then hastily drove off.

When we got out of the car, someone opened the carrying case and Esmé shot to the top of the nearest apple tree and hung there, howling. So our peaceful life in the country began by going to the village to buy a ladder so we could retrieve our cat. Meanwhile, the puppies tumbled out of the carton and scattered like autumn leaves, and we all ran around fishing puppies from under the barn, in the swamp, and stuck in the fencing around the chicken house.

In time, we had workable, heated kennel units built in the barn with good fenced runs, really quite professional. But our dogs never spent much time in them, because they preferred the house. My daughter, in later years, remarked once that we might have lived in the kennel and left the house to the dogs because with every sofa and comfortable chair filled with dogs, nobody had a place to sit down!

They were all house dogs, and even when we tried to rotate them we felt guilty at some of them being away out there in the barn at night. It was only when we had thirty-five that we used the kennels part-time.

THE SEVENTH WONDER

The homeplace is the greatest wonder of all,
the place where 'we can be ourselves,
without pretense':

The seventh wonder is different for everyone. But it is always the same. It is a home-place. It may be a walk-up apartment in the city overlooking a fire escape and well-furnished with soot from neighboring chimneys. Or it may be a mansion (although it does seem to come hard to make a mansion a true home). But it is the place, wherever it be, that men come back to after work, children come back to after school, and women come back to after Red Cross meetings, P.T.A., church committees, shopping or working at a gainful occupation themselves to help the family budget from withering away.

It may be full of tensions and anxieties, and it may be shabby. But it is a place where we can be ourselves, without pretense. Where we can confide our fears and worries to the members of the family. Where we can express our dreams, even if they happen to be impossible to fulfill. In this era of rapid divorces and much emotional instability, there are many unhappy marriages and disturbed children, I know this. But a homeplace is still an anchor. The whole family has a vested interest in the books, the old candlesticks from Grandma, the cross-stitched luncheon set (Mother's Day gift from the tomboy) and dozens of other things.

It may well be a homeplace is the greatest wonder of all!

A DIFFERENT KIND OF FREEDOM

Time passes, but the important thing is not in time lost but moments cherished. Gladys Taber describes here the untimed day:

I do not actually feel a year older on my birthday, now coming up on the clockface of time. I only feel a sense of the value of the moments, hours, and days that are yet mine....

My watch has been broken for a couple of months, and I have made a startling discovery with regard to time. I get along very well without being able to peer down at my wrist every few minutes. In fact, life moves along so easily that I have stopped going into the jeweler's and saying wistfully, "I don't suppose you could hurry a little?"

I have never known a jeweler who believed in hurry, certainly not my gentle old man. After all, he lives with clocks and watches going on like mad all around him; he can flick his tools and make a timepiece register any hour at all! So possibly, he comes to feel that one day is as good as another.

At first, I fretted considerably. And finally, a sneaking kind of freedom crept into my mind. I find it delightful to go to a tea party and just relax, visit comfortably, and never wonder whether I ought to be going home because look how late it is! I don't *know* whether it is late or not. And when an ice storm took down our wires so the electric clocks stabilized themselves at a quarter of nine for a day or two, I went happily ahead. We had lunch when we got hungry, and supper after dusk.

I found out that the washing does not have to be on the line at ten in the morning, and that it is rather nice to iron sometimes late in the evening.

Of course, I know that if a man has to get to the office and the children must catch the school bus, it would not work to be so unmindful of time. But it occurred to me that women might present themselves with an untimed day now and then and find just how restful it is to the hurried nerves.

I daresay, eventually I shall have my watch back and begin dashing around on a split-minute schedule. But I do think it must have been pleasant in those days before clocks were invented and nobody ever knew exactly what time it was! For after all, sundials mark only the hours that shine!

The heart has its own time. How incredibly fleet are the happy hours, and how leaden-slow the sad ones. The clock cannot hurry the sorrowful minutes a jot, nor clip the wings of the joyous ones!

Sometimes, I think we rush so, and we finish a schedule only to make a newer and busier one. We do not, ever, live deliberately and fully, for we haven't time. I know few people who go outdoors now and sit quietly for a couple of hours just looking at the miracle of spring. Sometimes, as we drive along the country roads, I see occasional figures stretched out in lawn chairs. But they aren't observing May, they are reading the newspaper or a magazine. They are like the people I have seen on the great beach at Nauset on Cape Cod who never hear the music of the tide because they have portable radios playing hot music!

It is good to have leisure, to walk in the September sun slowly, humming a small hum and picking a few wild dark-purple grapes. The old forsaken pastureland is a dream of yesterday, for surely it has not changed much since the women in early days came out for the same berries to make candles for the winter nights. Around the grey ledge, I may see the shy face of an Indian child, brown as a hazelnut. Then, Indians were friendly here, for these settlers were good folk.

The September moon belongs to lovers even more than the spring moon. Indeed, if we could fill a silver cup with that moonlight, and drink to the last pearly dregs, we should be young forever. For thc moon has a pure luminous mystery that makes everything beautiful, everything magic. The massed colors of early autumn glow in its light, all the little streams run silver, and silver rises the smoke from burning leaves.

There is as yet no taint of withering or death in the garden, in the field, in the orchard. The world is perfect, and the heart is happy.

The sky looks like a blue meadow full of gardenias, but the moon herself is a white rose. And down below, the old earth turns in her orbit under all this eternal glory of the heaven.

And the pale gold leaves begin to fall from the sugar maple.

A TRADITION TO INHERIT

Old houses have much to offer and in their offerings is an inheritance from the past, the 'good foundations to build the new world on':

Old houses have a special charm for me. They have a special lived-in quality, the sense of time having passed over them, they are steadfast. Fireplaces that have warmed generations have something a brand-new fireplace does not have.

Often in the flickering light from my own fire, I can see handmade shoes on the hearth being warmed, or copper-toed boots. Or possibly now and then satin slippers. The satin slippers would be very special since the folk who built Stillmeadow were simple folk, and worked the land.

Old houses were built soundly, built to endure. But now and then things happen to them. Our friends Lois and Burt Klakring were about to buy an old house not long ago. They were just ready to close the deal when the real estate agent took them down to the cellar to see the furnace.

"And one thing you can be sure of," he said proudly, "these old beams are as sound as ever." He took a penknife from his pocket and stuck it in one of the great foundation beams.

Whereupon, the knife sank to the hilt, soft

powder began to drift out, and the beam ominously cracked open. They all ran for their lives, Lois said. They made it, but it was a near thing.

So they got a modern house in the end.

With a modern house you begin the traditions, I feel, but with an old house, you inherit them.

Actually, in an old house like Stillmeadow, you always live both in the past and the present. The electric dishwasher purrs along while I wrestle with one of the windows which has to be propped open with a hickory stick, and which, once up, has to be hit with a hammer rested on a folded washcloth to get it back down. The vacuum cleaner swishes along an erratic course over those old wide black-oak floors with the wide unfillable cracks.

As far as Stillmeadow is concerned, I don't need to worry about its being too modern. There are limits to what a pre-Revolutionary house will endure from this generation. We shall go on the rest of our days jacking things up here and there, scrubbing the woodwork, painting old handmade clapboards, and waxing the antique furniture.

Many of the modern things are exquisitely beautiful—the glass, the silver, the linens, the plastics—and the colors are used so expertly. But the heritage of the past is lovely, too. Milk glass and cranberry glass and the old handmade sea-green goblets from that attic in Maine, and the pair of old French scent bottles with the delicate blue and pink flowers and the gold leaves—these are things to cherish.

The old maple four-poster with the holes where the ropes once tied, the chest with one pull missing, the pine combback chair—these are my friends whether they are in fashion or out.

And I feel the same way about other heritages from the past. Such as integrity and honor and faith in God, and love. Getting ahead, ambition, intelligence about material gains, these are nice and modern, but the old-fashioned virtues are good foundations to build the new world on.

Reflections

'THE VITAL FACTOR'

Love. Here Gladys Taber discusses many kinds of love, but decides that after all is said and done, 'it is better to love than to analyze':

In years to come we may know the answers to many questions. Now, every question that is answered seems to cause more questions to arise. But I think the basic answer to most questions is love, for with enough love, we gain understanding. And we are forgiven many mistakes we make if we have love.

"Mamma didn't understand, but she loved me." That is a good saying, and I have heard it often.

I suppose children grow up more in spite of their parents than because of them. The one vital factor is love, and neither children nor adults flourish without love. Love is to human beings as the sun is to plants.

The heart is a strange country, but the most important thing about the heart is that it longs to be unlocked. All of us, I think, go through life longing to have our hearts unlocked. But it is a difficult lock and so many keys do not fit.

There is, I think, only one way to unlock a heart, and that is to say, "I love you, I cherish you. Could you let me in?"

In any area of life, I believe love is a grace fully given, and if fully given, is likely to be returned. If even a wild bird momentarily in your hand can accept the fact that you care about him, how much more this is true of human beings. There are many kinds of love, in fact, I recently read a category of them. But I think it is better to love than to analyze.

THIS IS OUR DEMOCRACY

The families of America at suppertime, 'at home in the spring of the year,' have a special meaning for Gladys Taber:

Sometimes we drive through the valley past the little white villages. Men and women and children are out, the older folk raking or weeding, the children playing jackstones on the steps or jumping up and down in that purposeful aimlessness of children.

All over America, families are doing just the same, supper being finished. And at such an hour, I feel one can hold the whole of America in the curved fingers of a lifted hand. Surely this is our land—families at home in the spring of the year, and bountiful summer ahead. This is the meaning of our democracy . . . and let it never again be threatened.

HAPPINESS...A MATTER OF MOMENTS

Everyone seeks happiness, but those who find it are those aware of the golden experience of the moment:

Happiness is not a thing you can cut off by the yard or measure in chunks. It is a matter of moments when you suddenly know that this moment is special. A few such moments are enough for a long time. The trouble with most of us, it seems to me, is that we chase happiness so hard that when we find it, we have already rushed on looking for more. The truly happy person is one who realizes the happiness of that moment, or that hour.

To be happy, one must be aware. For instance, there is a moment when you catch your breath seeing a pair of cardinals flaming against a dark branch of pine. This is a simple happiness, an awareness of the beauty and mystery of Nature. The happy person says, "I saw the cardinals." The unhappy persons says, "Why don't they stay around? Why didn't they come before?"

Translated into other areas, it is the same. The happy person cherishes a golden experience, but the unhappy one wants it to last forever. It doesn't. It is like the marriages that break up, as so many do, because the excitement wears off and there are just two people living together. Glamour flies away, as the cardinals do. But the happiness of marriage can never be exhausted if both partners find new rewards in shared experience, in maturing companionship. No woman ever, I think, forgets the first kiss of her first love. But that comfortable kiss on the cheek after ten years of marriage is even happier. It has in it all the nights sitting up when the baby was sick, the times when there just wasn't any money, the quiet times when nothing at all happened.

I am sure many women would agree that happiness is that peck on the cheek at suppertime and the earnest inquiry, "Is everything all right?"

Maybe he doesn't notice the new hairdo or the new dress. But he wants to know if everything is all right. So this is a special moment, it is happiness.

PERSONAL RELATIONSHIPS

Here Mrs. Taber deplores putting the marriage relationship through the tests so often found in magazines. Marriage is a private world:

Advice to women continues to be handed out largely by magazines and books. We seem to be in an orgy of confessions and case histories. Can my marriage be preserved?; what is wrong with my husband?; whom shall I marry?; I have a jealous husband; I have a stingy husband; my husband does not speak to me for weeks at a time, what shall I do?

I have a secret feeling we do too much of this kind of thing. I especially deplore grading one's mate. I can always imagine a reasonably happy little woman getting a list and grading her husband and finding he flunked the test flatly! What, I ask, is going to happen to *that* marriage?

Marriage is a pretty individual affair and I doubt whether it can be push-buttoned successfully. Possibly I am just old-fashioned, but, like John Crosby, I cannot care too much if Mrs. A and Mr. B are one way or another about each other. I would feel it their business, not mine.

I wonder whether this preoccupation with personal relationships has spread over into private lives from the Hollywood stars' on-again-off-again marriages? If so, it is a pity we do not let the Hollywood greats have a little privacy in their lives off the screen. I am sure they would be grateful. They might even be more tranquil if people did not dodge after them every time they stepped from their front doors.

MY UNICORN

Although her friends inquire about her unicorn, no one has ever seen him except Gladys Taber. He arrives at Stillmeadow around lilac time to assure her 'there's still magic in the world':

When the lilacs bloom, I look for my unicorn. Yes, I know the unicorn is a legendary animal, but my unicorn and I do not care about that. We are quite real to each other, and isn't that what counts? He comes from the woods, usually at dusk, walks delicately down the hill, cropping the violets as he moves. When he dips his head to drink at the pond, his silver horn catches the last light. I met him first many years ago, on a night of full moon. I went down to the pond to watch the moon in the water, and at first I thought my unicorn was a flowering hawthorn bush at the edge of the woods.

It would be nice if it were a unicorn, I thought.

And so it was. I could even see his silver hooves as he moved down the hill. As he always has, he cropped the violets. Through the years, he has acquired many friends who ask, "Has the unicorn come yet?" But nobody has ever seen him except me. And, of course, I only see him at this time of year. He goes back to his own country, and where it is, I do not know. But he gives me assurance that there is still magic in the world when he comes in lilac time.

'THE HIGHER THINGS'

Twentieth-century American women subjugated to slavery? Gladys Taber describes this attitude as surprisingly medieval:

I heard a woman lecturer a short time ago saying American women were enslaved by household drudgery. Selling their souls, she said, when they should be pursuing the higher things in life. This was the time I lost my temper, which happens about once in six months. She went on to say young married women spent too much time on their children and their houses and fixing up for their husbands. At that moment, I could see the walls of the room turning a slow red.

For it seemed to me her attitude was medieval

—born in the era when only the low peasant classes did anything with their hands. The noble folk embroidered or chased deer. And she thought she was ultra-ultra modern! To make a home beautiful, to create a good family life, seems to me a job as important and dignified as any, and there is no reason why pushing a vacuum cleaner is incompatible with thinking about Plato or Aristotle or Parker's *Aesthetics*. The truth is, I thought, saying nothing while she monologued on, that any job is according to the person performing it. My mother, for instance, was never a career woman—she had no college degree, she was a housewife. But her heart was wise, her intelligence was keen, and the memory of her is still a shining thing for many people that I know about. And if this lecturer, with her shaggy fierce look, had met Mother and they had conversed, the odds would have been entirely Mother's. Inside of a short while, Mother would have found out what was really wrong and, without seeming to, would have suggested something to ease the bitterness that sharpened the attack on the enslaved American wives.

FAITH

Gladys Taber argues here that it is with faith that we prevail over unhappiness; it is through belief that we keep our courage:

Faith is a strange and wondrous thing. All winter we see the lilacs leaning against the blizzards, gray, and lifeless. Nothing could look more dead than a lilac bush in January. It is only a bunch of sticks. The only thing alive about it is the chickadee swinging on a doughnut hung on a branch. Quite casually the miracle begins. There is never a moment when we can say, now the buds have begun to swell. As love ripens in a good marriage, the lilacs turn the tight glassy buds into small spikes, and then into visible purple. And then, in May, a flowering time comes.

Walking to the mailbox in the snow, I reflected that one has to know the change of the seasons to believe in spring when it is January. This also, I thought, is true of the heart. The heart can endure its own winter, provided there is faith in spring. All of us have times when trouble seems to be more important than anything else. Sickness and death make us wonder why we keep on. Almost everyone, I think, has had moments of wondering whether it is worth it. Economic

hardships can wear courage down, too, especially when there are young children to take care of.

But life has its rhythms as the seasons do, and the most bitter times may be followed by an easing. It is very important, in winter, to remember that spring is coming along. The new tulips will blossom in dark splendor, the lilacs will pour forth a headier fragrance. In the spring of the heart, too, we have gardening to do, planting seeds of goodwill, helpfulness, and faith.

Planting is an act of faith. The small envelopes of minute hard particles do not have the slightest suggestion of the tender sweet corn, the snow peas, the dark and juicy beefsteak tomatoes that are somehow in them. They lie in this earth, secret and still, and then suddenly one morning a green mist seems to come over the garden. Fragile and delicate, tiny etched lines mark those string rows where Jill moved back and forth so patiently.

Presently, we go out and pull the silvery savory scallions and the rosy crisp radishes–and the miracle has begun again! As I snip the tips of the first scallions, I am always feeling that one of the most hopeful things about mankind is that we go right on planting when the season comes, despite bombs, wars, world crises. There is a basic faith in mankind that planting is a secure thing.

MORALITY MUDDLE

Here Gladys Taber describes the endless gyrations that moral judgments can entail and how much simpler it is to end one's confusion with a cheese soufflé:

The moral universe is a fine phrase and I sometimes wonder what, exactly, they mean by it. Ordered it must be, for the seasons go in perfect order, the roses come in order and the migratory birds even migrate in order. When the thermometer drops a degree at a certain point, rain must become snow. This is order. As far as mankind is concerned, whether the universe is moral or not is debatable. Morals are a sometime thing. To be moral in Connecticut has nothing in common with being moral in the communal life of the jungle. Morality consists of following the pattern you are brought up to follow. And it changes so. It was moral in the Pilgrims' time to cheat the Indians, to lie to them, steal from them, ambush them and take their own land from them. We respect the Pilgrims for their bravery, their fleeing to America and many other things, but not for their moral relationship to the natives.

Today in my valley it is not moral to gain advantage through trickery over anybody. We even have ideas about traps and how many fishhooks should go on a line.

As far as wildlife is concerned, I cannot feel there are either bad or good, moral or immoral birds and/or animals. I think this is perfectly silly.

The predatory blue jay who snatches the best suet is only following the blue-jay pattern. The cowbird lays her eggs in other birds' nests, but maybe it is because she cannot figure out how to make a nest for herself, who knows? or is she dilatory and doesn't get to nest-making until all the good apartments are already taken?

I always end my thinking in confusion and decide to make a cheese soufflé for supper, as I understand that very well.

'THE STARS STILL SHINE'

Even when grief raises a barrier between people and their happiness, 'there is still joy to be had in the immeasurable gifts of life':

Life renews itself, no matter how much we may suffer. Whatever beautiful and precious we may have is always ours to keep. Losing one we love is possible only if we let it be. Death and disaster, separation and sorrow seem sometimes so much larger than all else, but they are not. Over the deepest scars in the cutover forests grow young, green, ferny thickets. And these do not blot out the memory of trees once standing there; they are nourished by the roots. But I know people who would say, "Leave the blackened stumps and burn off the new green, it is desecration to do aught else." They are wrong.... Death really prevails only when we deliberately walk with him.

Even if life seems too difficult at times and grief gets too intimate with us and death raises his umbrella between us and the sun, there is still joy to be had in the immeasurable gifts of life, if we accept it. I do not mean to be a Pollyanna, for I always thought she was a tiresome person. But I think one should never lose awareness of all that is lovely.

When my own mother died, there seemed to me to be no answer to anything. For a time, the only universality was death.

And then I remember walking in the dusk along the quiet little street toward the house now so empty and meaningless. There was light enough from the sky to cast the lattice shadow of leaves on the walk. The sound of the river was steady and swift, and the air smelled of sulphur from the mills beyond the river. As I looked up, a delicate petal of moon drifted into the tender blue, and all at once I thought, How beautiful God made the world! How wonderful that the stars still shine! And I was comforted.

Precious Moments

'PERFECT MOMENTS'

There is a time, especially for women, when suddenly a lifetime of varied experiences becomes distilled in the mind. A moment like this is to be treasured:

There is always one moment in a day when I think my heart will break. Such a moment, I think, all women have, and men too, when all the meaning of life seems distilled and caught up and you feel you can never, never bear to leave it. It may be when you turn and look down a blazing autumn road, or it may be when you see your house under great ancient trees, or it may be in the city when you look up at a towering apartment building and see one light and think "that is mine." It may be any one of a number of things, according to the circumstances of your life.

But there is the moment when all the heartaches and sorrows of your life suddenly diminish and only the fine brave things stand out. You breathe sharp clean air, your eyes lift to the eternal wideness of the sky.

Anybody has moments like this to store up, but some people are too busy adding up their frustrations to appreciate them. And yet, all we need is an awareness of the beauty in life to make us richly content. My definition of happiness is just the ability to garner the perfect moments.

STILLMEADOW SEASON SAMPLER

In the seasons of the year, Gladys Taber finds spiritual nourishment:

January is a drama in the winter season. Driving against the pane comes the sleet, and wild is the sound of the wind from the fierce heart of winter. The sky can be black as anthracite, and the drifts roll under it.

Dark comes so early these days. We seem to have practically no afternoon. Around four-thirty the snow has a blue tinge, and the sky has a faint pale glow. The woods are dark charcoal, and most of the birds finish their feeding and begin to settle into the thick, fluffy white pines by the swamp. The chickadees that have been singing all afternoon utter a few last Dee-Dee-Dees and snap up a few last sunflower seeds.

The color of winter is pure and lovely: the long, darkly blue shadows, the purple stalks of the briery bushes, the glistening white of clean snow, the pale amber of shell ice where the little brooks walk in summer. The meadow is latticed now with the pattern of dark branches and the great timeless trees lift intricate patterns against a still sky.

March is for buttoned jackets and woolen gloves, for wild wind and a trumpet sun, for sharp exciting nights with scudding clouds and a white moon sailing. March is for considerable sneezing, for muddy paws, and for scouring and scrubbing.

April in New England is like first love. There is the tender excitement of gathering the first snowdrops, the only symbol of life in the deserted garden. They are the lyric expression of music

to come—as the symphony of lilacs will surely come—because I am picking the cool delicate bells of this first flower.

I like to get up and dash to the garden to see what the rhubarb is doing and then carry my breakfast tray to a sheltered sunny corner by the well. I like to eat outdoors even if I have to wear a sweater, and Jill says I will eat out even if I have to wear mittens while I cut my bacon.

Moonrise silvers the sky as we put the house to bed. And May, like Byron's love, "walks in beauty, like the night of cloudless climes and starry skies."

White lilacs in the moonlight, white fire of moonlight over blossoming apple trees, white little house under the great sugar maples—and Little Sister and Holly waiting by the door—we are deep in spring!

June sun is like a Chinese lantern, warm and richly glowing, but not yet too intense. It is life-giving, and it is dreamy.

June is the singing month. Rambler roses everywhere, over white picket fences, over gray stone walls, climbing old well houses, blooming on lattices in old-fashioned gardens. The whole green countryside is laced with shell pink, ivory white and rose red. The sky sings, too, such a deep tranquil blue. I think I can hear the horns of elfland faintly blowing as I go out to the Quiet Garden to shell peas.

In New England, June ripens into July so easily that it takes a keen eye to notice the change from early summer to full, lavish midseason. The nights are usually still cool enough for a casual fire in the fireplace, but around noon there is a breathless dazzle in the yard and garden, and the afternoon is slow and dreamy.

There is something really wonderful about a hot summer night, I think, as I turn the light out and the moon comes in, steeping the room with silver.

Some days the air is like a flannel blanket dipped in steam. Swimming makes life endurable; a cold fresh stream is one of the nicest things God ever made.

Now, in September, a few delphiniums bloom, the herbs are luxurious and the polyanthus blossom and the clematis is budding. The little garden is even quieter as summer ends, and lovely for suppertime use.

If anyone now asked me what happiness is, I should say it is a September day in New England.

Now is the time to go out to the woods for butternuts and hickory nuts and hazelnuts. The upper pastures are gray-green and tranquil, the deciduous trees flame against a sky as soft as the breast of a dove. The old graystone ledges are warm, the light is golden on the fallen burrs.

Some of the days in November carry the whole memory of summer as a fire opal carries the color of moonrise.

The cockers and I run to the door as soon as we get up; they lift their soft noses and sniff, then dash out to see what might have crossed the yard in the night. I breathe to the very bottom of my lungs. Yes, it is one of those days—those last and lovely gifts of New England autumn!

The first snowfall is worth having winter for... First, a few tranquil flakes float down, then they come faster, and with purpose. The old graystone walls silver over, the swamp wears a mantle whiter than foam. The pine trees on the slope begin to cast feathers of snow from their branches.

Seasons flow one into the other, today moves inexorably toward tomorrow and we cannot keep even the most enchanted hour. World events shape different unknown destinies for mankind. Nevertheless, these abide: love, friendship, faith in God. Thcsc armor us against the transitory aspects of life on this planet.

'WHAT WOULD I DO IN CALCUTTA?'

Dreams are wonderful, even if they don't come true, for as Gladys Taber says, 'without a star, the sky can be very dark':

It is strange to think how our dreams change. When I was growing up, I cut out pictures of yachts and planned to live on one of the most elegant. It took growing up to make me realize I could get seasick even at a movie which showed a boat rocking. I dreamed of being a Red Cross nurse, too, without knowing that I suffer so over a bruised paw that I would never have been worth my salt. In emergencies, I am fairly good, but as a nurse, I would have worried the patients to death. I would always have had every ailment known to medicine, and my temperature would have risen with that of anyone whose temperature I was taking.

When my daughter was born, I dreamed that she would fulfill all my dreams, up to and including being an actress as great as Shirley Booth has become.

Now my dreams are more fitted to an adult life. I dream of travel, but do not wish to leave home. I would wish to get back in time to feed the dogs and look at the moon rising over the swamp. For the truth is I get homesick if I even go away overnight, so what would I do in Calcutta? I would worry over whether the roses had aphids and whether Holly was brooding. I think it was Scott Fitzgerald who first said that one gets vulnerable as life goes on. The more you love a person, the more vulnerable you are.

And so, as you have children, you begin dreaming of a golden future for them. A good many children, I think, suffer from trying to fit into parents' dreams which are not at all their own. It is better to let the children have their own dreams, and to follow them.

But in any case, people without dreams are unfortunate. We all follow some star, and without a star, the sky can be very dark!

‘A PERSONAL STAR TO STEER BY’

Here Mrs. Taber finds friendship her greatest guide in bereavement:

I have never known anyone who did not need a guide when facing the unknown. The great, indomitable explorers set forth in Arctic wastes with compass and a bearing on the stars. They usually had maps, often incorrect, but they were something to go by! The Himalayan climbers take human guides, Sherpas who know the frozen heights of ice. Columbus navigated by stars and the maritime instruments of his age. The primitive people wandered from place to place according to signs and portents.

In our personal life, we are guided all along the way. What young parent attempts to raise a baby without Dr. Spock? Well, in darkest Africa and in the Arctic, they have not heard of Dr. Spock, but I am sure they will before too long. I hadn’t heard of him either, when my baby was small, but I had guidance from the family doctor. We are guided in education, rightly or wrongly, but still the course is laid out and we follow it.

In our country, we have marriage pretty well charted. It is laid out as an obstacle course, with the bad parts provided for. Marriage continues to be a personal adventure and may fail, but not for want of guidance.

It occurred to me, after Jill died, that I suddenly had absolutely no guidance to this undiscovered country of grief. I was just in it. I had faith and prayer, but I really had no training at all.

At the time I first faced the fact that I was to be alone, it did not seem to me I could develop any skill in managing anything. It was, in fact, quite hopeless. My life seemed as purposeless as a drifting sailboat. But I had a strong sense that I was now meeting the most difficult learning-time of my life, and it might be I could learn a little. I needed a personal star to steer by.

I found it in the assurance that I had a relationship with life because Jill was still an integral part of it. This cannot be explained; it is felt. My guide was to be the same steadfast love of the past years. And so I was not alone, although I might be solitary.

Working back into life, I found the greatest guide was friendship. There are two reasons for this: The more I shared the lives of friends, the less I concentrated on my own. The world opened out, wide and interesting. Secondly, I found it eased my heart to spend love (of which I seemed to have a great store). I had time, now, to make new friends, too, which had not been possible during Jill's illness. And sharing the happiness of others, as well as trying to help with sorrows, gave me a new sense of being a part of life itself.

Friendship is related to love, and if love is the bread of life, friendship is in the same package. And friendship is a very good guide. In fact, it seems to me the world situation, as I write, is partially due to a lack of willingness to make friends, to care about other people, other lands. This characterizes the rulers of many countries. If the nations could work at making friends, there would be no threat of war, ever again.

I could not rewrite history, of course, but I could let friendship be a guidepost for my life.

NEW ENGLAND BOILED DINNER

6-lb. cut of corned beef, brisket or rump.
Place in cold water to cover, add ½ clove garlic and 6 peppercorns.

Bring to boiling and cook slowly, skimming when needed. This takes about 4 hours as a rule. Test for tenderness with a fork. When tender, remove it and add to the stock the following:

6 carrots
3 large yellow turnips, cut in halves or quarters
4 small parsnips
8 small peeled onions

Simmer 15 minutes, then add 6 medium potatoes, peeled and cut in quarters, and a head of cabbage cut in quarters.

When the vegetables are tender, return the corned beef to the pot and reheat.

Serve on a hot platter, garnished with parsley. Serves 6-8.

Gild the lily, if you want it gilded, with horse-radish sauce. (Beat sour cream with freshly grated horseradish or prepared bottled horseradish. If you use the prepared, add a little lemon juice.)

No doubt it was the New England boiled dinner that gave the early folk energy to fell trees and conquer the wilderness. It has been around a long time, possibly stemming from the English boiled mutton. It still warms the cockles of the heart on a snowy winter night.

LOBSTER STEW—
THE NEW ENGLAND WAY

2 lobsters (at least 1 pound each)
½ cup butter or margarine
1½ qts. light cream (top milk will do, if necessary)
2 tbsp. or more sherry
seasoning to taste

Boil the lobsters for 15 minutes (in sea water if you can get it). Remove to a dripping pan and, when cool enough, split open and remove the meat. Do not skip the coral and tomalley (red roe and green liver). Press the juice from the feelers. Put the lobster meat, tomalley, roe, and juice from the dripping pan into a pan with the melted butter or margarine, and stir constantly until the butter or margarine covers everything

except your apron. Cover and let stand several hours. Then heat the cream in a double boiler until it is hot but not boiling, add lobster meat and juice and seasonings. Watch the salt if you have used sea water.

Let cool. Then put in the refrigerator for 24 hours.

Reheat, check the seasoning, and add the sherry. Serves 6.

Lobster stew, like clam chowder, needs to mellow. Or, as we say in my part of the country, it has to ripen.

Serve this in a big tureen, preferably ironstone, for the creamy color is just right with the pink-rose of the stew. Add crusty French or Italian bread, a green salad, and plenty of hot coffee. Nobody will want dessert. You may offer them fresh fruit, crisp crackers and Camembert cheese, if you must. But don't use a strong cheese. This is not time for the robust Cheddar after the rich savory lobster!

INDIAN PUDDING

4 cups milk
3 tbsp. yellow cornmeal
1/3 cup molasses
2 tsp. salt
1/2 cup sugar
1 beaten egg
butter (size of a walnut)
1/2 tsp. powdered ginger
1/2 tsp. cinnamon

Scald 3 cups milk and stir the cornmeal in slowly. Add molasses and salt and stir until thickened. Remove from the heat and add sugar, egg, butter, ginger, and cinnamon. Pour into a buttered baking dish and place in a 300 degree oven. After 30 minutes pour 1 cup of milk over pudding and bake for 2 1/2 hours. Serve with rich cream or vanilla ice cream.

This is an old-fashioned dessert which does not resemble what passes for Indian Pudding in some restaurants. It is moist and light and calls for second helpings.

BAKED STUFFED CLAMS

1 7½ ounce can minced clams
½ cup clam juice
2 tbsp. melted butter
¼ cup seasoned bread crumbs
¼ tsp. each: basil, marjoram, thyme
½ tsp. lemon juice
salt to taste
few drops Worcestershire
grated cheese, Parmesan
paprika

Drain clams, reserving the juice. Mix butter, crumbs, the seasonings, and add ⅓ cup of the clam juice. Add this to the clams. Spread mixture in clean clam shells, dot with butter, sprinkle grated cheese and paprika over.

Heat in moderate oven (350°) for 10 to 20 minutes. Let cool slightly before serving.

This makes 6 clams; better double the recipe.

You make these up ahead of time and freeze. It is an easy and delicious first course, but is even better as an accompaniment to cocktails or tomato juice. I first had this on Cape Cod, and not one of the ardent clammers knew the clams came from a can! We ate on a porch overlooking the ocean on one hand and the prettiest Cape Cod garden I know. A bevy of quail and four mourning doves attended outside the screens.

CRANBERRY TEA BREAD

3 cups sifted all-purpose flour
4 tsp. baking powder
1 tsp. salt
1 egg, beaten slightly
1 cup milk
2 tbsp. melted butter or margarine or Crisco
1 cup cranberries
¼ cup fine granulated sugar
½ cup chopped nutmeats (walnuts or pecans)
1 tsp. vanilla

Sift dry ingredients (the first 3) together. Add the milk and butter or margarine to the beaten egg and add to the dry ingredients. Stir until well blended. Put the cranberries through a food grinder or chop in electric blender. Add the sugar, nuts, and vanilla. Add to the batter and pour into a greased loaf pan 9″ by 5″ by 3″. Bake in a moderately hot oven (350°) for an hour or until the bread draws away from the sides of the pan and is browned on top.